# Planes, Trains and More

By Sue Graves

People travel often.
They travel in many ways.

People travel through air on an aeroplane.

People travel across land
on a train.

People travel across land on bicycles.

People travel across water
on a ferry.

People travel into space
on a space shuttle.

# Ways to Travel

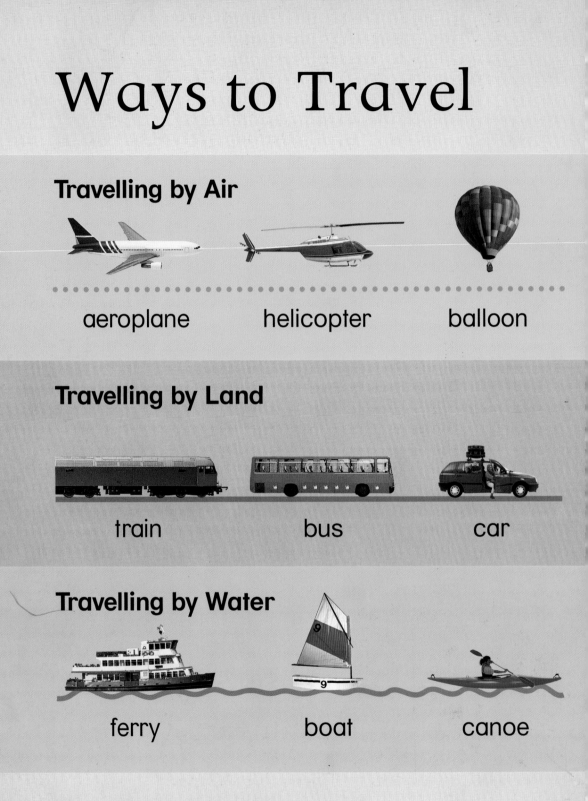

**Travelling by Air**

aeroplane     helicopter     balloon

**Travelling by Land**

train     bus     car

**Travelling by Water**

ferry     boat     canoe